WALKING LIBERTY

Other volumes in the series:

Eve Names the Animals by Susan Donnelly
Rain by William Carpenter
This Body of Silk by Sue Ellen Thompson
Valentino's Hair by Yvonne Sapia
The Holyoke by Frank Gaspar
Dangerous Life by Lucia Perillo
Bright Moves by J. Allyn Rosser
The House Sails Out of Sight of Home by George Mills
In the Blood by Carl Phillips
The Eighth Continent by Don Boes
Plums & Ashes by David Moolten
Living at the Epicenter by Allison Funk
Understory by Michelle Boisseau
Reading the Water by Charles Harper Webb
American Spirituals by Jeffrey Greene

The Morse Poetry Prize
Edited by Guy Rotella

JAMES HAUG

Walking Liberty

THE 1999 MORSE
POETRY PRIZE
SELECTED AND
INTRODUCED BY
ALFRED CORN

Northeastern University Press
BOSTON

Northeastern University Press

Library of Congress Cataloging-in-Publication Data
Haug, James, 1954–
     Walking Liberty / James Haug ; selected and introduced by Alfred
Corn.
         p.   cm.—(The Morse Poetry Prize ; 1999)
     ISBN 1-55553-409-0 (alk. paper)
     I. Corn, Alfred, 1943–   .   II. Title.   III. Series.
  PS3558.A75644W35   1999
  811'.54—dc21   99-35275

Designed by Ann Twombly

Composed in Weiss by Graphic Composition, Inc., Athens, Georgia. Printed and bound by Versa Press, East Peoria, Illinois. The paper is Glatfelter Offset, an acid-free sheet.

MANUFACTURED IN THE UNITED STATES OF AMERICA
03   02   01   00   99   5   4   3   2   1

for Jack, Nicky, & Alix

ACKNOWLEDGMENTS

Thanks to editors of the following journals in which these poems
first appeared, some in different versions:

American Literary Review	"Salvage City"
American Poetry Review	"The Layout"
Artful Dodge	"Continued Nice"
Brilliant Corners	"Mystery Groove"
College English	"Poverty Mountain"
Crab Orchard Review	"The Class War So Far"
Crazyhorse	"At Thirty," "Dock of the Bay"
DoubleTake	"On the Rail"
Gettysburg Review	"Fourway Sunshine," "Garage Songs"
Green Mountains Review	"Turpentine," "After Winston Link," "Along the Old Jericho Road"
Massachusetts Review	"In the Missing Town"
Mid-American Review	"August," "The Following Day"
minnesota review	"Levitt"
Ploughshares	"25 at Dawn," "78s"
Quarterly West	"The Trick Is"
Willow Springs	"The Peace"
Witness	"Trade Wind," "Rocks My Pillow Too"

Some of these poems were published in a limited edition, letter-
press chapbook entitled *Fox Luck* by the Center for Book Arts,
New York, in 1998.

My thanks also to the National Endowment for the Arts and the
Massachusetts Cultural Council for their generous support.

Contents

Introduction: "Afoot with My Vision"

A character in James Haug's *Walking Liberty* named Mike Gray climbs to the top of a small-town water tower and, after being coaxed down from it by a policeman, is asked why he did it. He says, "I needed some altitude. / I thought I could maybe see where I lived." I'm guessing this is also what Haug wants to do in his second collection of poems. He has a Whitmanian ambition to catch America in the fact, to see it whole, as from a certain altitude. An impossible goal, but the reach that exceeds its grasp is also an American trait and helps explain an undercurrent of disappointment counterbalancing our culture's official optimism. In his updating of Whitman's *kosmos*, Haug has trained his lens on the micro- instead of the macro-level, becoming the latest chronicler of the island called Paumanok in *Leaves of Grass*. If contemporary America consists above all else of suburban communities shading off into farmland, Long Island is a good research laboratory for the national essence, with the additional advantage that it has a history as old as the earliest colonies. Stray facts from that history creep into the fabric of these poems, not all of them especially exalted. "Levitt," for example, gives a thumbnail résumé of how the prototypical tract housing development came into being, Haug's account of it a strange blend of humor and foreboding.

Several of the poems narrate their subjects through the actions of an alter ego named Walter, whose last name, never given, is probably not Whitman. Even so, he is one of Whitman's heirs, one of the roughs, but come down in the world in direct proportion to the decline of American prospects over the last century. Haug's Walter sets out on his roadside tramps for reasons more practical than Whitman's, specifically, the recovery of lost hubcaps that can be sold for ready cash. Another of his income-producing activities is menial work in a supermarket, a central shrine in our consumer culture. On the other hand, no reason is given for Walter's nocturnal explorations of empty houses in "The Layout," but the mention of hypothetical sleepers in the poem ought to summon up Whitman's great dream-poem of the same name, and we come to see that Walter has more on his mind than paying the rent.

James Haug's flair for apt and surprising visual observation leavens all these poems, so much so that I recalled Abe Warburg's much quoted assertion that God resides in the details. Those noted by Haug seem too vivid and inevitable to have been made up, yet they are often couched in the optative or hypothetical mode: "Let it be or look this way," he'll say, or, "If this were so, then we'd see this." What reality doesn't provide, the imagination will, that's its job, as the poem titled "'Long Island Landscape with Imaginary Mountains'" implies. In it Haug echoes a regret of the nineteenth-century painter William Sidney Mount, who felt that Long Island should have included, as a painterly convenience, a mountain range. "Revery alone will do when bees are few," Dickinson tells us, and Haug is fully able to fill in the blanks left by a deficient reality, as he so eerily does in "In the Missing Town." This might amount to nothing more than a conjuring trick if it didn't remind us just how much American experience unfolds around a central vacancy, an emptiness at the core of things that objects and interiors can nevertheless evoke, as they do in the paintings of Hopper, who may be one of Haug's influences.

Absence is the downside of American readiness to discard the trammels of history or convention, and Haug examines the other side of the coin by musing on our sometimes perilous freedom in the title poem, which refers to the design of the half-dollar minted during the Depression. Liberty in this avatar is not static, but instead strides along in her loose skirts, a rising sun in the background. She is the updated version of the dime and half-dollar issued in the more affluent and sedate teens of the century, which showed Miss Liberty's head only. Haug may or may not be aware that the model for that earlier Liberty was Wallace Stevens's wife Elsie, as cast by the sculptor Adolph Weinman. Somewhere between the breeze-blown grasses of the open road and Stevens's spectral interiority, the poems of James Haug have been conceived. May he prosper.

ALFRED CORN

xii

WALKING LIBERTY

Fourway Sunshine

It doesn't matter, I say, even if I lose my mind.

You can't lose your mind, says Mike Gray, you replace it
with a negative mind, a mirror mind
in which words are spelled backwards, in capitals,
like *ambulance* or *emergency.*

It's the end of August. Everything falling echoes itself.
There is a black moon, a man raking grass at midnight, shell-
    shocked,
trimming hedges by floodlight in the nation of Long Island.
In a corner of the Elwood Diner, behind a pyramid of empty non-
    dairy creamers,
a cab driver from Montauk is fashioning
wampum out of coffee cup lids to buy it all back.

There are chunks of history under all this, says Gray, slowly
waving his hand before him,
the ratcheting of crickets rising from yard after yard.
In 1664, Captain John Scott, empowered by the Duke of York,
became President of Long Island, the first recorded
use of that title in America. John Scott, explorer, rascal,
the first realtor. He worked for the Dutch, the English, the French,
    the Indians.
He fended off the advance of Puritan rule. He rode a magnificent
    white horse.
He returned to the village with hunters at the end of the day,
oxcarts in tow loaded with pheasant and plover.
The trail can't be far. We don't know exactly where.

Mike Gray is an explorer too.
Streets to get lost in: Elgar, Elman, Eldredge, Elmar.
Here a dry sump bed.
Here a sump of green-black water in which he'll wash his hands.

Here a vase of permanent flowers.
                    Mike Gray rises
ceremonially from a squat, flipping the hair out of his eyes.
What I like most, he says, is the sound
of my own voice, and then he says nothing more.

On top of potato fields houses stand in rows like matchbooks,
an impenetrable geography though I'm in it.
A King's Dairy milk truck coasts to a stop along the curb.
It's the last bottle of milk. The insulated milkbox lid
whucks closed, like a ghost door, in the land
where night links everyone into a vast chain of ownership.
Upon waking we will all, collectively, drink our milk.

And I'm drinking mine, though it's stolen,
the milk running rivulets down my chin and over my shirt,
blots of it purpling under Mike Gray's black light.

And when Mike Gray tripping on a hit of fourway
has finally been coaxed by the police
down from the Greenlawn water tower he was perched on,
the detective pleading routinely through a bullhorn
as if it were real life,
his processed voice crackling, nearly human,

and Gray has been folded
gingerly into the back of the cruiser,
a cop asks him what in hell
he thought he was all about standing up there
squinting, with a hand shading his eyes, like Geronimo?
But Gray is an explorer. He refuses to lose his mind.

Through the half-open window, pupils dilated, he says:
"I needed some altitude.
I thought I could maybe see where I lived."

Salvage City

Everything ends up by the side of the road.
Walter walks off the lengths between exits,
a canvas sack slung low from his shoulder.
With a stick he spears at the ground for junk.
Bitten chunks of tire tread, crushed empties,
cellophane, coffee cups stained with kisses.
Fourteen thousand steps a day, every day.
As a kid he scavenged hubcaps from the weeds—
mock wire spokes with knockoffs, baby moons.
He scared up a kind of income this way,
polishing hubcaps with Turtle Wax
until his face came clear in the shine.
A dozen a dollar he hawked at the junkyard,
where the terrain, evolving, included him.
Then he'd snoop among the woe of stripped cars,
a good boy, guest of Salvage City.
New wrecks at the gate sank hub-deep in mud,
windshields webbed with cracks, with hair
(Look, a blonde, the owner once said),
the folded metal a relief map of impact.
There it was always turning dark, a twilight
of grease, of ground steeped in oil, sludge
pressed by the worry of boots and tow trucks,
churning, as if the place were a huge machine,
hardly running, on the verge of breaking down,
the crusher, the forklifts, the orderly
rows of bumpers, engine blocks, axles and shocks,
the front office lit by a gooseneck lamp,
the archaic calendar stuck forever on July
with the unlikely nude in a sailor's cap,
penny gum-balls, pine tree air-fresheners,
the owner's hat, and his famous dirty dog,
all part of the machine, all breaking down.

Walking home, Walter could finger singles
crushed in his pocket, sizing up the road
glaring before him: a foolish river of cars,
accidents on the make, grinding things up,
big wheel of the sky turning, dumb stars,
fevered yellow glow of mercury vapor—
all of it lighting the way for Walter
where even now with a sack he's on the lookout.
The wide road ahead glitters with hubcaps,
with speed, with money to be made.

Norfolk & Western

Near Fringer's Mill a boy's
    hunched over a kerosene
lantern. The night's so

dark he could be praying.
    How lonesome
must it get? The dirty

weight of steam-clouds hangs
    over the doomed
village. The miracle is

how much darker the lights
    of town make
everything beyond it.

Rabbit Brown gathers
    lilies by the track.
A little song for Harold

who lost three toes.
    A comb for Greta
whose cat is deranged.

If you follow
    the bridge out of town,
if you cross it

into the starless night,
    take this coin.
The magnetic flagman

begins to wigwag.
    Hester holds her teacup
steady for the 9:05.

78s

I've covered hundreds of miles in search of
the perfect song—records
often so ruined they sound buried
as if they were being played
under the floor. Along with 78s,
Stanley's Old
Furniture Store sold miniatures: homunculi,
chairs for mice, golf carts and threshers,
a pair of Guernseys
housed in a matchbox. I studied these
as a distillation
of size, an enormity I could pocket
and take with me. The relationships
their placement described said very little,
though as dust settled year
after year a story had emerged. Bankruptcies
and long evasive phone calls with bill collectors,
brothers who stood up
after a cup of coffee and never spoke
again. In the hills I've heard
lived the purest singers, miners
who came forth crying "You Are My Sunshine,"
fiddles that groaned like the last day
of fall, like an elevator descending
a dubious shaft. Out of gas
in a mountain town, Dock Boggs sang up enough
for supper, breakfast, and his tank.
Getting down the mountain was the easiest part.

Walking Liberty

It's almost half a Walking Liberty now.
The relief's fingered down, the knurled
edge smooth, shadowed as if
by hatch marks, one for each hand

it's passed through before coming to me.
Minted in the Depression, 1936,
the story goes this four bits stopped
a bullet, or deflected it.

Above the good Lady's outthrust arm
a gouge the size of a .22 slug
is bitten off, so that the burden of
the word arcing over her head vanishes.

She looks ready to step from the coin.
A black-rimmed sun at her feet is rising.
Portable ruin. Eagle with no perch.
The man was no hero who owned it.

Did he stand on a corner at midnight
thumbing the coin as a blizzard's first flakes
melted unseen into the dark
blue wool of his pea coat? A charm

for better pay, for fair weather ahead.
Stranded in a bus station in Elmira,
did he tap it idly on an armrest, a tiny
improvised Morse code, a way to

ward off the defeat he read in the other
passengers under yellow terminal lights
who dozed sitting up in coats and galoshes?
To make the night pass, did he buy a pint

of Wilson's bourbon, so that by the time
he was rolling away in the back of the bus
and dawn was coming up over Route 17,
he was crooning "Make the World Go Away"

in a baritone creaking from disuse?
The coin's what he'd hold up in a bar's
half-light, the thing that came between him
and a company goon's .22,

a clairvoyant glint in the eye as he bulled
about deliverance, the wisdom of idleness.
Death stepped down to him and brushed by,
inspiring the old chill, as clean

as cold air on the back of your neck
after a haircut. Dropping the coin
in his empty pocket, he swayed outside.
It's the last thing he would lose.

The Trick Is

Beyond the supermarket, beyond the liquor store,
    beyond the broken glass
throwing back glare at the height of noon,
    beyond the rain-washed
gullies gouged into the face of a dirt bank,
    Walter thought he heard
a quick pair of wings rustle among tall weeds.
    The least breeze spooked him.
In the dream he had last night, a young boy appeared,
    drinking an Orange Crush
in patched pants, and sat down, warning Walter:
    "By nightfall you'll be dead."
He didn't like the news, but what could he do?
    He collected shopping carts
left for dead over three flat acres of free parking,
    jammed one cart into the next,
and pushed them all at once in a long chrome train
    back through electric doors.
He stamped cans of peas with tiny adhesive price tags.
    He placed old milk in front.
With a sandwich, Walter crouched on break, on the
    edge of the loading dock,
and squinted hard up the dirt bank where crows were
    conversing, black as print
against the stark blue sky. He studied the weeds.
    The trick is not to ignore
what's around you, read the signs, and get paid.
    He bit down on his sandwich,
the wings of death surely fluttering nearby.

Mystic Concrete

My job was laying down concrete.
I remember a mockingbird flitting
fence-post to fence-post, mocking me,
placing a tentative order in the air.
It went on song after song—despite
the bits of gravel I chucked—pitch
perfect, trying every bird it knew.
Each morning that year I hitched
across the Niagara Frontier,
a name that calls up the colonials
who saw the place and kept going.
I swore at every passing car.

I began a song I knew by heart
about trains, about someone to whom
the singer is forced to say good-bye.
The wind hurled back its complaints
and I went on with lyrics having little to do
with me, which made me sing them.
After all, it was the songs that mattered
as I worked, selling the days—
how each song rose up unique from
the last, stolen, wholly original,
clarifying each perch from which it came.
How all those songs compose one bird.

Garage Songs

It's a killer, the guitar hook on "Little Girl"
by the Syndicate of Sound. It gets under your skin
and tugs you back to the radio for days.
But the singer's malignant little laugh is the key,
the gleeful cruelty of it, a demented grace note:
You cheated on me, but it's nothing
other women haven't done before. See, I'm laughing!
And the singer on "Dirty Water" means it when he
says, "I wanna tell you a big fat story,"
even if the story's so big he can sketch in
only a few lines of it before the harmonica wails.
He's alone by the river, the doors are locked,
the thieves are out of work, and the water's black.

I regret I can't find Bobby Fuller's "I Fought the Law"
since it sums up youth so well—you fight and you lose.
(On finding Fuller's body, the police said
he'd swallowed gasoline. But it never added up.)
The record must have slipped through a crack somewhere,
an old barn floor I've forgotten. Therefore, it's best
never to be sentimental over these things.
They're only 45s; forgive their scarred fidelity.
Or as Arthur Lee concisely put it:
"You wake up in the morning, find your boyfriend dead."

Jackie Brenston's "Rocket 88," recorded in 1951,
is considered by some authorities to be the first
rock'n'roll record (though I suspect
the first rock'n'roll song, if there can be such
a thing, was recorded earlier even than 1951
by someone like Big Joe Turner or Louis Jordan
or by someone using a driving backbeat
in a garage in Tulsa, of which no record remains).

That's Willie Kizart on "Rocket 88"
playing electric guitar through an amp with a cracked speaker
which gives the song that growling fuzz tone—
for the fuzz, for the right accident, thank Willie Kizart.

Once, a small blue transistor was all it took.
I had the beige earphone with the clear plastic plug,
like a hearing aid, which it was, pulling in
the music of New York City. I kept the antenna extended
from under the blankets to pick up the signal, tipping
the radio this way and that when static broke like surf
over the airwaves, washing out the DJ's elastic chatter,
after which, clear as winter stars, came a chorus
of something so far gone they played it only at night,
an epiphany, edgy, and utterly disposable.

Finally there's "Roadrunner" by The Modern Lovers,
anthem to loneliness, highways, and radios, circa 1972.
It endures recklessly, with the same obscure origins
as the best garage songs, songs looming suddenly
out of nowhere like little tornados and just as
quickly vanishing. It's about the place we find music:

in the dark, alone, with the radio on:

driving late at night with the radio on because
it makes you feel not so alone
when you're out there driving past midnight, alone
and restless, with nowhere to go,
and the music makes it tolerable to be there,
even beautiful, moving along a moonlit highway
late at night past darkened shopping centers
and lunar parking lots frozen under crime lights,
nowhere to go, but possibly beautiful, and perhaps
instead of going somewhere you are where you're going,

that every chord, every wheel-turn
is your destination, your arrival, that driving alone
at night with the radio on is a matter of always
                arriving.

25 at Dawn

Clock a few miles east on Jericho Turnpike—
how new asphalt levels the ride.

Consider too the foot-thick concrete slabs
(poured in the 30s or earlier)
we used to drive on, the road beneath the road.

Before that, plank:
two parallel rows of hemlock, four inches square—*sleepers,*
laid in three to four feet apart,

upon which eight-foot planks were placed unfastened.
A mixture of coarse sand, fine gravel, and dung

formed on the road a hard surface
which sped the delivery of produce and goods and pushed
the reach of commerce farther east.

Beneath the planks, an Algonquin trail,
footpath from the East River to Montauk Point—

Fugitive landscape.
                    The sun is rising
over a flea market spread across the rolling flats
of a defunct drive-in,
mute speaker-poles poking up like stubble,

wind shaking down the corrugated steel panels of the deserted
    arena.

Hard to name it, a place that's no place, so populated,
    and unpeopled.
Nowhere to walk, and nowhere to walk to.

After the developer slapped together enough houses, he came up
with a solution: name the town after him.
We lived in the map fold, in the pocket of the Northeast.

So it was that a chickadee
with its hooked song
awakened me thirty-five years ago.

Today, as I look for an old girlfriend's house,
the road beneath the road carries me along.

I heard she's a parole officer now.
That house sold:
                it's all painted yellow.

The Class War So Far

Under a blank coastal sky Walter slouches
near the water, hands in pockets,
and toes the frozen
discarded husk of a horseshoe crab.
Nothing's more ancient. Not even the terminal
moraine banked up the shore. Tide-worn
shards of glass pepper the beach like arrowheads.
Behind him stand squat fuel storage tanks;
behind them, one-story shops
muscle in shoulder to shoulder on Main.
Tarred pilings ringed with sea ice
lean out from under the dock they support—
a working dock, vacant since morning.
A port where coasters once unloaded
double casks of pickled tongue, firkins
of butter. Pewter and rifles.
Here a still life has composed itself:
embedded in the wooded hillside across the water
sits an occasional distant white house
where live people of impossible means.
A Private Beach sign fastened to a crumbling
concrete stanchion warns Walter off.
Friends settled here way back, toting homemade
brooms and chairs, veering off the Indian
paths, breaking camp, making real estate.
The problem of America remains: Who owns it?
And Walter's: What is he doing here, alone
with the day off, in the middle of the week?
He could be a late birdwatcher snooping
among coves and ruins,
Audubon observing gulls as they swoop
breaking mussel shells on the rocks,
or a tourist looking for colonial graves—

"Where are the stones to mark the bones
    Of those who die in Oyster Bay?"
The road he drives out of town curves north
along the inlet and teeters across
a dwindling spit of sand, straight for
that distant hillside, where the sight of two cruisers
posted at a clapboard station slows him down.
He U-turns at the silent picket gate
and watches in his rearview a cop watch him.
A beautiful woman sails by on rollerblades.

Turpentine

With a coffee can of turpentine
and a dirty toothbrush
I'm scrubbing down a carburetor.
I would have been done sooner
but I stayed out all night, smoking
in a potato field, waiting
for someone who never showed up.
My own voice startled me at first
when I sang to myself,
so clear it was, and shaky.
I kept walking. A green veil of
light ruffled the sky above
the power plant. Stacks blinked
against the dark. Turbines groaned.
Mechanics say, Don't force it:
Let the bolt find the thread.
I woke behind a hedge and saw
a green sedan creep away
and a parked Dodge catching fire
like sunrise, like her face
when she steps out of the dark.

Poverty Mountain

Along the old main roads, long grown over,
cellar holes from last century still gape.
It's at best half secret what's happened
even if ferns soften the look of the place.
On the floor of one cellar a stone hut
stands, with a huge gray slab on top, a roof,
looking like an altar or burnt-out manger.
There's something that tells us keep going,
the walls charred. But scattered over
the ground are beer cans, a pair of panties.
And across the plain face of a flat stone
a crude heart's been drawn with charcoal.
Signs of life.
       A little farther up the road
lies a grassy intersection—ghostly,
but calm enough for the two of us to stop.
Here, a mule-drawn wagon limped heavily along.
A whorehouse worked behind the feedstore.
A young man from out of town stayed at the Inn
where those fat pines stand. He says he wants to
bring back an inventory of Stetson hats,
of which this town is said to make the best.
For tonight, he'll rest. Through the trees
he can hear the clank of a trolley straining
up the hill, right past serene pastures,
even if the woods have taken those too.

At Thirty

           I used to call it fox luck
when a fox lit across the path of my lights,
flickering red in the road then gone.
Sometimes, coming home from work, I saw two,
because then I needed twice the luck.
Those nights I'd drive around an extra hour
on roads I hadn't seen before (for there
were many and I thought I had the time)
and stop for a beer. Under a hooded lamp
a few farmhands would be shooting pool.
I'd lean there and drink, as if I were
actually on the way somewhere, wanting only
to stretch my legs, to regain my bearings.
Make it a local joint called the Seven O's.
In the pauses between records I would hear
the cash drawer shut, the cars on 116
winding out past the bar and the Dove's Nest,
past a large field of ripening corn
and the house at field's edge, where the man
sinks into the habit of his chair and sleeps,
and the woman thinks she hears something stir
outside in the dark among the corn rows.
And the child will awaken many years later
to find most of it gone, his own face now
gone slack and usual facing himself, perhaps,
in the webbed glass of a barroom mirror.
He will think that place was once his home,
or even an idea of home, now squandered.
Let him slap down that quarter for eight ball,
the same quarter he has tried for hours
on the black pay phone in the back, the phone
that won't connect the call for the number
he keeps dialing, the number he knows beyond

reflex, though it's that too, the number
as deep in his memory as the farmhouse
which lies at the edge of a broad field, where
the man who looks like his father, like him,
will not answer. And the path that ran next to
that old house, the path that shines fatally
and vanishes behind the tall stalks of corn,
is empty now, but for the darting shadow
of a hungry fox called Luck, who stops,
looks over its shoulder, then keeps running.

August

When I say
   a yellow Chevrolet stuck in the August corn
it isn't purely material. There's

metal, it's true, enameled surfaces, immovable
   chrome, the exhaust still warm,
a brittle shudder when the wind strokes

the ears of corn, how they sway
   unlike metal, unlike
almost anything else. There is

that. But not purely. It's more about
   the quality of light at the end
of a season, a deepening orange

infusion evening by evening, not the end
   of the year, a rehearsal for it,
so we may feel things are ending

before it happens. When in August I dug
   fence-post holes for my friends
they were still married. When our work

was done he praised the seductions of
   the physical world, the fence
that gave form, the proof of our labor.

I rubbed the new hardness in my hands
   and dusk came over the freshly
posted split rail for the very first time.

Nothing had ended. I drove with a woman
   on Moody Road. She wanted back
the elk tooth her father presented her

after a week of hunting in Montana.
    Lying, I said I lost it. Twilight blurred
the slanted lines of her face inside

the car parked on the edge of a cornfield in August,
    where even the yellow leaves
could not retain the light,

in the absence of which material hides
    before the naked eye. But the car never
was stuck, was not a Chevrolet.

It's that I like the sound of *yellow Chevrolet*,
    the Ls and Os, and how
conjoined with *August corn* it sounds

American, possible only on this ground,
    how *stuck* nails it all
into place, a fear of the soul at rest.

I drove the woman home. I drove home.
    We gave up our homes. There is a stasis
called August, where half-light stalls,

where night yearns beyond a split-rail fence
    and a hand holds on,
where the rumor of a frontier lingers.

Levitt

Then came trucks, with crews
aboard each one—one to pour

foundations, one to frame,
one to solder plumbing, one

to help you call it yours.
Buyers stood all day in line.

As soldiers they dreamed of home.
They stood in the dust of the vanishing plain;

they slept in their cars.
The streets were called Shelter and Vale.

A dead end Levitt named Wisdom.
A factory narrative of quarter-acre plots,

of covenants and radiant heating,
of wide streets for speedy evacuation.

No man who owns his own house, he said,
has time to be a communist.

The social critics called it barracks—
a source of eerie recognition.

Planes circled for aerial shots:
Capes packed side by side

on streets flowing
like the swirling lines of a thumbprint,

a neighborhood spiraling outward.
So the veterans regarded themselves.

Where to go? What to do?
As soldiers they were used to waiting.

Tiny Island After Three Days' Rain

Cows nuzzled the blue pickup parked on a knoll,
tiny island after three days' rain.
How silent the river became as it rose.
Son House was alive in Rochester.
I was studying the footing where a bridge once began
and the road overrun by woods.

In a downtown steak house I discovered
a poster for the True Sam Patch.
Glacial melt spilling over the Niagara escarpment
had cut the Falls, which Sam Patch,
the Jersey Jumper, leaped in 1829,
and over which two years earlier the *Michigan*

tumbled with a cargo of worthless dogs.
This seemed important, as if one's life
were the arc of someone else's leap,
and the tiny island just got smaller.
The car I bought from a junkyard ran

two and a half years. I coasted downhill
with the lights off past starlit vineyards.
A miracle so many of us lived.
For years at a clip it was like a fight
about to happen, like nodding
off while driving the service road

that loops around the old airfield. The high
school teacher drinking black wine
tottered like a man on stilts among his neighbor's
tomato vines. You see, fall was upon us,
a cold snap signaling more to come,
and a bible salesman just then knocked at the door.
Let him in, I said. He burned the couch

dozing on it, so I took the cigarette
from his fingers. It's not a likely place
to stop, the little farm town that clings
to the English version of its name. A jilted
mycologist played stride on a tack piano.
The weather was always November.

Always a hippie giving away mongrel puppies
outside the diner where hunters wolf donuts.
A young couple perched on highhat stools signed
promises they'd written out on napkins.
The rest of us tabulated our bills on the air, rehearsing
new magic, making coins vanish, then us.

In the Missing Town

They've removed the benches to keep the dropouts
moving. They removed the final dive.
A dancer worked the stage, a white scar down her belly.
On his arm the manager wore the blue tattoo
of a woman strapped with barbed wire to a cross.
Everyone has his mark. Now where
the town was is another way of living.
I'm in the old neighborhoods, what's left,
walking slowly because the evening is slow.
The grid of streets is the same, the house numbers,
the drawn curtains. But I see better
what I remember than what's really out there.
The junkie who bought it on Hill Street
still lives. The widower behind a dark window is
smoking his pipe. He hears the distant evening
train pulling out of the station. He places
a fedora squarely on his head. Where is the aspen?
Where is the subterranean garage,
the hissing radio, the frozen bolt giving under the wrench,
the slack-jawed automobiles without engines?
I build the town all over again. It's up to me.
I plant missing roses and tend the final dive.
Before dawn I unlock the ancient depot doors.
A train lurches away from the platform, west for the city—
the sky bleached orange, erasing constellations.
I wave my flashlight down the dark street.
In the morning, the one-armed man—I don't know his name—
pries the lid off a can of car wax with a penknife.
Honeysuckle is tangled in the chicken-wire fence.
A rotting black oak shades this half of the street.
With the stump of his left arm he clamps the can
against his side while the right hand applies
a damp cloth smeared with wax to the already

shining finish and begins rubbing in small clockwise
circles that corkscrew into white nebulae.
He brings a deeper radiance to what he works.
He's on that other street. Keep him waxing all day.
Let him drive side streets steering with one knee
when he drinks from a bottle of beer.
Let him tip his lost hand like a fin out the window
to feel the pressure of the wind against it.

The Layout

Breaking into a house is not simply what
   Walter will find or how quiet he must be.
A half-moon's rising above the monotony of roofs,

above the water tower near Depot Road.
   The layout echoes every house around it.
Here's the cyclone fence, the strip of lawn

anchored by a clothes line and a crab apple tree.
   The back door opens into a kitchen.
Paper moth, crayon skyline, black toy parrot.

One chair's pushed back from the table where a half-empty
   coffee cup sits, a faint trail of rings detailing
the placemat like a chart of lunar phases. An ashtray

with one cigarette left to smoke itself. The tinny
   insect scratch of a clock radio
tuned to all-night jazz. It isn't so strange.

It could be his house, the way it's done.
   Put out a hand. Isn't there a lightswitch there
beside the bookcase? Isn't that photograph a dog

dressed as a cop straddling a motorcycle?
   In one house, guns, blue bottles on a sill,
dime-store prints of pheasant and mallard, in another,

an atlas with countries in it that no longer exist.
   From an upstairs window he can make out
the pocked earth of the town dump

where small blue fires flare at random and die
   and the yellow light of a single dump truck,
like a new star, ascends an artificial mountain.

If there were sleepers now in this room, he
    might lean close to see dreams flicker
beneath the eyelids, the blurred stripe of sweat

above the man's upper lip, the woman
    pensively touching her fingertips to her chin
as if something's been taken away.

If it were morning he might see dust swirling
    over their bed in a shaft of sunlight,
the dust which, a mattress salesman once explained,

is composed of so many specks of sloughed-off skin.
    Body ash, he called it.
As if Walter himself were slowly burning away.

"Long Island Landscape with Imaginary Mountains"

Lost for at least an hour I cannot recognize
a single house.
What does lupine in a meadow look like?
Is it true that
after forty years plywood comes unglued?

Inside the convenience store
a clerk in a red smock jabs her finger
at Hempstead Turnpike.
"If there's no God, who made all this?"

The sky's so flat it needs relief—

I had in mind a place wherein
a twenty-foot tall milk bottle dwarfs a cow
and a dormant windmill
looms between a locksmith and a tile showroom
and houses are patch-job summer
conversions banged together by refugees.

Instead postwar Capes, tricked out, share
an uneasy vernacular.
Doghouse dormers, pressure-treated decks, sliding
glass doors, raised roofs.
What were once saplings now make honest shade.

Island of Shells: quahaug, periwinkle.
I'm an outsider in a Drug-free Zone.

Looking west in the afternoon as a bank of clouds
built darkly upon itself
it came to William Sidney Mount what was missing—

a mountain range right here.

Continued Nice

That night we camped outside the city.
Supper at sundown and I was hungry again.
Lanterns strung along the flat
roofs of the tallest buildings swayed
on a tiny wind off the plains.
I could hear from my bedroll the last
song wrung from a concertina,
stray dogs nosing over garbage cans.
Since I'd never seen it I pictured it
as my city (a mistake):
trolleys grinding up and down the tracks,
how the crust of hot bread breaks in my hands
as I walk to work in the morning,
the candy shop with a small teller's window in back
where I buy sticks of marijuana
and gloved hands take my money.
Intricate commerce, block upon block.
I kissed a girl beneath a billboard.
I pawned my guitar so I could buy
drinks for everyone. I'd have traded
the log under my head for one more slow drag,
for a look at the funnies
before we had to tear it all down.

Sentimental Catalog of Flight

A B-52 six miles up scrawled a contrail
the length of Long Island, four streams of vapor
like a dream of parallel rivers, feathering out.
Picture, as Walter did, the anonymous
pilot inside the hard globe of his helmet,
ice webbed over the tailfin—

mornings when under his fingertips
window glass shuddered—

Closer to earth Piper Cubs buzzed so near
their props were intimate, even
lonely as they crept east for the water.

Sometimes a biplane trolled back and forth
towing ads for Guy Lombardo,
for figure-eight crack-ups at Islip.
Chugging at antique speed,
it was the sky's quirk, fragile as a basket,
as if accidentally
it had slipped through a rip in time
like a postcard fifty years late.

In a vacant lot a Cessna sat
held fast by berry snaggle and creepers,
site of some unrecorded crash,
the wings bleached, out of true.
Walter forced the door to see what the pilot saw—

subdivisions, the long scars
of the Long Island Railroad, the LIE, as he tilted
hard west for the mainland,
strafing the beaches Robert Moses made.

What eats at Walter still is what
happened one late afternoon

when a biplane in a tailspin
spun cruelly in a beeline for the earth,
for Commack at least,
and nobody saw a thing or pointed.

Was it out of gas or just a trick?
After a sudden buttonhook over Vet's Highway
would it swoop back into the air?

"Okay," said Walter, like a pilot in the movies
choking a last message into his mask,
"This is it!" This is it, he said to himself,
earthbound in the backyard behind
Acme Supermarket, unable to see
beyond the house in the next lot.

Dock of the Bay

The day I heard his last song I was in Woolworth's.
I can't think of what on earth I was looking for.
The floorboards creaked. Sand dragged under my shoes.
From a bin I lifted a white candle and scratched
my initial with my thumbnail along the side
then laid the candle back down with the rest.
Months before, Otis Redding's plane had gone down.
There came news of other deaths, an undeclared war.
The clerk went on shelving ceramic blue angels—
he was keeping an eye on me. The register closed.
I drifted past toy guns, drapes, packages of seed;
here was all available, a nation of goods;
here I thought I'd find what I always wanted.
Another clerk behind a red badge scurried past me.
Over loudspeakers came the whispering of waves
and the resigned bass line, then Otis singing.
A large convex mirror fixed high up on the wall
made the whole store look like a world on sale.
I was dreaming of the other coast, the one Otis sang of,
the coast where you arrive when it's all over
and nothing's going to change. I stood out of sight
and slipped a thin notebook inside my jacket.
Who knew if loneliness would ever leave me alone?
I stepped into the stunned air of the parking lot
with my blank book, and my American secret safe.

On the Rail

It's twelve degrees,
so help me. When I shut my eyes I'm hitting
a four-wheel drift on New York Avenue.
At five this morning I sprayed ether
in the carb of two-nine, the cab with
the floating backseat and the bad air.
A monkey wrench leached my hand of warmth.
The jumpers I threw back in the trunk.
In a cloud of breath Charles unscrewed
a thermos and poured a little into
my empty styrofoam cup. No steam.
Scotch'll keep you, said Charles, Scots himself.
Into his own cab, the one-five,
he heaved himself behind the wheel, slung
his false leg (the right one) over
the transmission hump, the *News* beside him
folded around the red-plaid thermos.
By noon he won't know or hear a thing.
Now I'm on line behind him, on the rail,
staring down his tailpipe, idling . . .
There's no correlative for ice, well maybe—
I saw the knife glint in a fare's hand one night.
The thing was to pretend. A strand of
Christmas lights spiraled down a conifer
like a painted vortex. No one was home
across the street. The gases of the cosmos recombined
right over my head. I gave him my money.
An old woman muttering curses in Norwegian
rattled empties down the sidewalk.
Now I shut my eyes and there's no more road,
only distance, the tires going bald,
whispering Mayan conspiracies, hydroplaning.
I can smell the stale ether of cigarettes.

38

Nothing could possibly happen to me now.
I've had a Mars bar, a black coffee,
and a hard roll with too much butter.
Over the radio the dispatcher calls my number,
calls me back to the world to drive.

Trade Wind

The world's not really realistic anymore.
Walter's two daughters don
the underwear of an immortal superhero.
They want to read some creep his rights,
burn him in the Big House.
Walter wants to finish their bedrooms
by winter—do the trim, prime and paint.
Not even his house looks realistic.
It's more of a boat now, plying
the brooding weather of upstate New York.
Something like the wind brought him to this:
carpenter, shop steward, navigator.
It's all makeshift. Hammer, and hope it holds.
Before dawn, hands free of the rudder,
Walter charts their position:
Orion leans back against the fall sky, waggishly
hitching his tool belt.
But at this hour not even the stars play fair;
the House of the Seven Sisters fades.

Mystery Groove

Who could tell he was missing
   two fingers of his right hand?
The chord voicings, a little

sparse, were agile and fluid. No
   one knew looking at him that
he'd wasted a decade playing

trad for drunks in a racetrack
   saloon. Incessant circular
arpeggios left us nearly

undone. Every summer night
   brought jump cuts, a glittering
zeal frothing at the edges,

a pinch of thrash-metal,
   tuberculosis, an
expanding sonic palette.

Aloha Danny, she said,
   play it lowdown. After that
it was "Peacocks" on a daily

basis, a thumping bass
   propelling ensembles half-
cocked across the desert, pillars

of thorns, stints that kept him
   raspy and well-fed. The guy
on vibes made his name riffing

off "Harlem Nocturne," on which
   he built a living—a slim
reed. A whipsaw trombone. And

on pocket trumpet, Snake Boyd,
    whose out-of-tune passages
were exuberant, a skit-

tering dialogue. He was
    looking for a little quiet
place in the cosmos, moping

in space with a dollar
    thirty-seven, some organ
fills, some hollers.

The Peace

Dogs go on barking and nobody shuts them up. A brick wall has baked all day in the sun. As evening comes on, men lean against the wall, the heat pressing into their backs. They smoke hard little cigars, waiting for something to disturb the peace. At the bus stop, women from the frozen food plant are stepping down. There's the heat of the bus pulling away, the heat of the valley enclosing them all. . . . At night, a small canal dug in along the edge of town begins to reek. It runs behind the bar where a woman sits down heavily on a stool; the beer bottle hisses when the bartender twists off the cap. The canal leads out of town, under the main road, through a rocky field, uphill to its source—the shaft of a deserted salt mine. An acrid odor of gas seeps out of the earth. On Friday nights, when the mine was going, workers parked their cars in a wide ring and drank in the headlights' glare. The sky was brilliant. Now everyone keeps away. In an apartment built onto the back of a house, a woman's failed to awaken her husband, so she leaves him there on the couch. She shuts off the light in the kitchen and pauses at the screen door. If nobody's there to stop them, the dogs will go on like this all night.

Rock'n'Roll and Cruelty

When I heard George Freeley mowed
the head off a live cat
I only half disbelieved it. And though

I never said so later, I was there
when Freeley leveled Ray Murphy.
As they walked beyond reach of each other

across the mashed football field, Freeley spitting,
Murphy, six three, dreamy as he
looked out over Freeley's square head,

it was perhaps dawning on Murphy how much
punishment his overgrown body
would have to take for years to come.

I heard Murphy sigh when over
his shoulder he studied the bobbing heads
of two hundred kids stoked for blood

fanned out in a wake behind him
like a legion of junior Romans,
a sigh, had we known it, that said

he was taking the long view,
he was fixing on a point somewhere
way off in the future, a town perhaps

where the light didn't die
and the mayor would declare Ray Murphy Day,
a town beyond even the best of us.

Freeley threw the first shot and kept coming.
Murphy backed up in circles inside
the ring our bodies naturally had formed

as Freeley, blue-eyed and flushed,
knuckles shredded, blackened Murphy's
other eye. Even when someone tripped

Murphy, Freeley hunched down
and slugged his ear. No one thought he'd stand.
And as Murphy staggered backwards,

held up by the crowd, we took our shots,
working over whatever was left.
The next day in a pizza parlor, I stood alone

at the jukebox as sun slashed through the window.
I couldn't tear myself from the music
no one else was listening to—

not the nervous cashier with defoliated eyebrows
rolling a half dollar over his knuckles
or the girl spelling her name backwards

against the sunlight
or the boy hunched in the corner hiding his face
as he sucked the straw in an empty cup—,

the music taking me on as I scanned the jukebox
for the letter and number: "Gloria" by Them.
Gloria climbing the stairs, Gloria knocking on the door.

Outside the traffic backlit by the dying sun threw
shadows across the parking lot.
Gloria, I said, and the song spelled it out.

Along the Old Jericho Road

Runoff pushed the river up its banks.
Dark was soon to fall. I carried
what I could, loaves of bread,
snapshots of famous horses, an illegible
tract on the discovery of cobalt.
I hummed an old gospel hymn,
along the Jericho Road. In a circle
I sat crosslegged, singing with
other cracked voices. What a friend
we had—the moon cradled
in a pine grove. We were singing
it turns out for dawn to break
because we were hungry and small
and the hymns were a comfort.
In moonlight we rose and came upon
a clearing. That was me, walking away
from the others, dropping my pack.
I heard rumors among the cypresses,
a hoot owl, distant fireworks.
There was a light that faltered
where a city should be, a fallen tree
bridging the river, open country
on the other side, to which I fled.

After Winston Link

In the brown weeds near Fringer's Mill
a boy's hunched over a lantern, catching moths.
A 4 × 5 camera's set fifteen feet behind him.

The old mill wheel where he's crouched
has slipped its axle. In the distance
a Class Y locomotive shoves a freight north.

He traps each moth in his cupped hands
then releases it to the dark. Most are
wood moths, an inch wide, and common.

He can find them orbiting the lamp
outside Goggin's hardware store
where new brooms lean all night in the window.

Or they flurry around the naked lightbulbs
at the depot, until a train
pushes through, pulling them up in its draft.

Even in daylight they're common:
one hides in the folds of his mother's coat,
one flies out when he kicks a rotten log.

But a luna is hard to come by. It loves
only fire and the moon. It stays aloof.
That's why the boy now has lifted the shield

of shaped glass from around the lantern wick:
he's only got a minute or less before
the kerosene's gone and the flame dies out,

before the Class Y enters the frame,
at which time the camera will memorize
the starkly etched grain of the mill wheel spokes,

the startled trees edged by a silver flash.
One of the last great steam locomotives
will bristle in the background as the boy ducks

and a luna moth, rarest
of all moths, hovers within reach.

The Following Day

Gary was only running out to buy waffle mix
and blueberries for his son's
breakfast. Sure, it was one in the morning

but since he works the swing shift he has
little opportunity to make such runs.
Besides, it's impossible to sleep when he gets

home that late from work. He's wired up
yet he must keep quiet. Everyone else
in the house is asleep. That means

no loud music, no sudden home repairs.
No late phone calls to friends since they're asleep
probably too—anyway, he's too

old for that. Too busy to sit in the Somewhere
Else and nurse expensive drinks
and watch strippers go to work. Or to linger

over the *Racing News* in the T-Bird Diner
and observe a gash in the pre-dawn clouds turn pink,
to the right, above the sloping rise of sand

where as a boy with his pals he dug in with hands
and feet in order to climb, and for every two feet
he went up, the sand dropped him

back a foot, the ascent sapping him, until
breathless he could stand at the top
and witness the last of a pasture that was

only then being converted into cul-de-sacs. Give him
the sweet small taste of corruption when
he sits on a stoop with a fresh bourbon and ice

before the birds wake up and the only sound is
the cubes rattling in the glass and maybe the shush
of a far-off car passing—how that sound hangs on,

the duration of it, the decay. There must've been
a point when he entered the life he would never
wish to trade. A moment when he last felt

dawn settling on his bare arms and a spark
flew from his cigarette when he pitched it
against the sidewalk, his debts small

and fleeting, like the phantom taste
of acid eaten decades ago, a flavor of being
sixteen and in trouble and hitchhiking

half the night in search of a beach party,
but then the beach was dark, the tide way out,
and the shore so rocky

it was as if the water had all but dried up
and the party like a wandering herd had migrated.
So when he returned home with the waffle mix,

his family coughing in the street, he was
surprised too, he explained the following day
to the police, who thought it was funny

a house going up that quick and he's gone
at one AM. Why, he could be heard repeating,
why would a man burn down his own house?

Rocks My Pillow Too

From under a rotting gazebo
I hold out my hand
and let it fill with cold rain.
While the rest of us keep dry,
Walter, out of work,
plants his feet in soaking ground.
He reeks of gasoline.
A brown quart bottle of cold beer
snug under his dungaree jacket,
with his name stitched above
the pocket, Walter,
because he says dungaree,
because the world, he says,
slips by degrees away from us,
tilts back his face drenched
with October rain
and sings a song for nobody at all.
A random song, song for failure,
made-up, stolen,
Cold ground was my bed last night,
Rocks my pillow too.
Song for sand, song for lime,
song for the burning guitar.
Walter, bowlegged, straddles
the imagined shivery horse of death,
digging his heels in deeper.
He drags a soggy mechanic's rag
across his face, swaying to the tune,
rain falling straight as wire,
when a hard whoop at last
breaks out from beneath our rotten roof,

and somebody begins to clap hands
then somebody else—
because this is what you must do
in order to keep time.